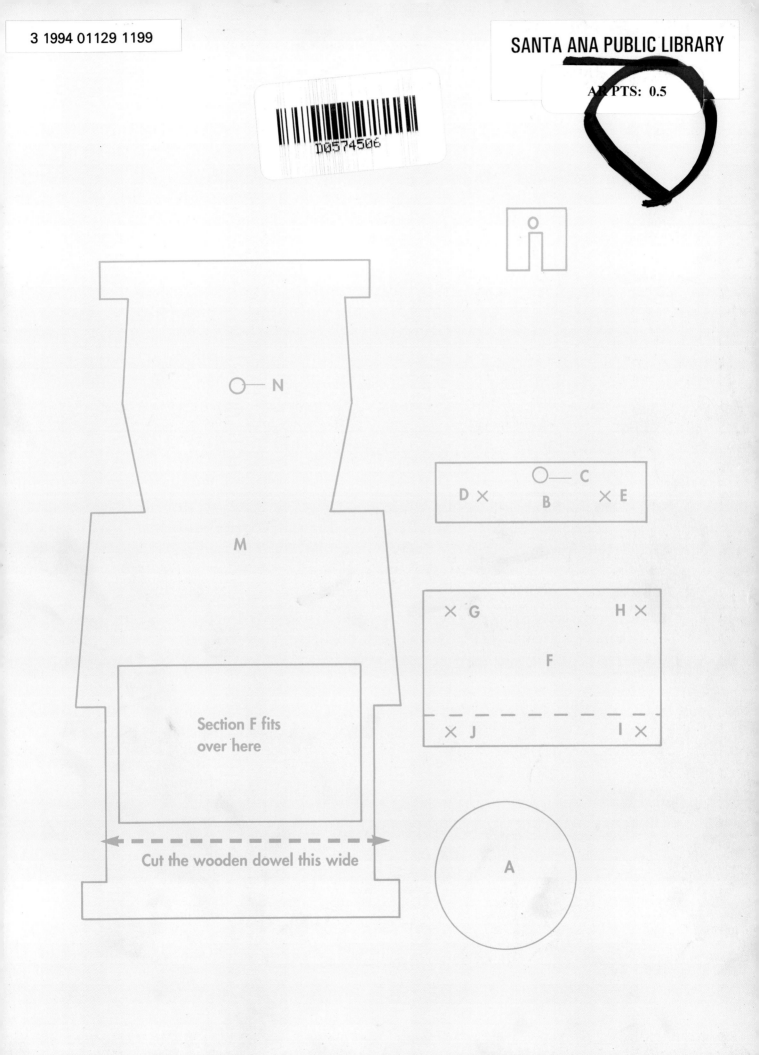

O

N

M

Section F fits
over here

Cut the wooden dowel this wide

D ×   ○— C   × E
           B

× G   H ×

F

× J   I ×

A

CARS, TRAINS, & MOTORCYCLES

CHRIS OXLADE

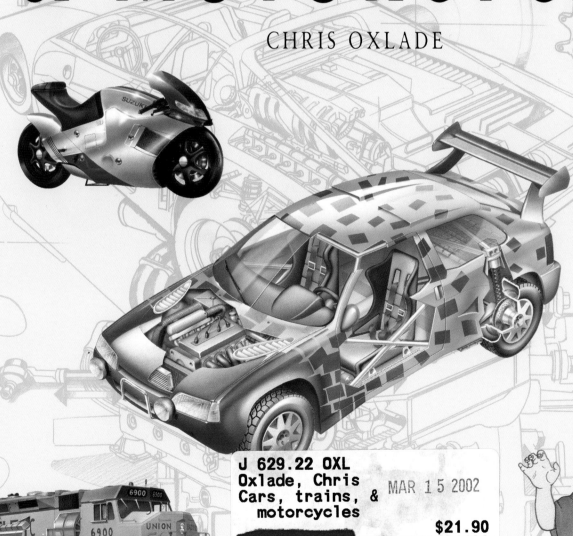

COPPER BEECH BOOKS
BROOKFIELD • CONNECTICUT

CONTENTS

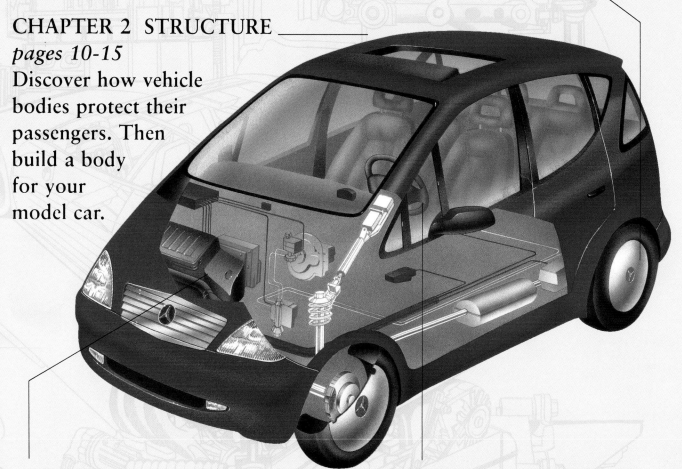

INTRODUCTION

Land vehicles come in all shapes and
sizes, from the biggest train to a
scooter that can be packed into the
trunk of a car. But almost all vehicles
have wheels. They all need engines
to drive them forward, and they all
need brakes to stop.

Look inside cars, trains, and
motorcycles and discover the science
that makes them work. Then test your knowledge by building a
model – just like designers of a Formula 1 racing car.

To make the projects, you will
need: thick and thin cardboard,
corrugated cardboard, rubber
bands, a craft knife, scissors, white
glue, strong clear glue, paper clips,
acrylic paint, a felt tip pen case,
beads, wooden dowel, a bendy
drinking straw, stapler and
staples, thin wire, and tinfoil.

Model car
project box

Science experiment
project box

© Aladdin Books Ltd 2000

Designed and produced by
Aladdin Books Ltd
28 Percy Street
London W1P 0LD

First published in
the United States in 2000 by
Copper Beech Books,
an imprint of
The Millbrook Press
2 Old New Milford Road
Brookfield, Connecticut 06804

Cataloging-in-Publication data is
on file at the Library of Congress.
Printed in Belgium
All rights reserved
ISBN 0-7613-1165-3(S&L)
ISBN 0-7613-0841-5(Trd Pbk)

Editor
Jim Pipe

Science Consultant
Dr. Bryson Gore

Series Design
David West Children's Books

Designer
Simon Morse

Illustrators
Ian Thompson, Catherine Ward,
Simon Tegg, Alex Pang, Gerald
Witcomb, Don Simpson, Aziz
Khan, David Russell, Ron
Hayward, Graham White,
Peter Harper, Ross Watton,
and Simon Bishop.

Picture Research
Brooks Krikler Research

THE SCIENCE OF MOTION

Cars, motorcycles, and trains are like all moving objects. To get around, they must accelerate (speed up), keep their speed, and decelerate (slow down).

They often need to change direction, too. But they will only change speed or direction when a force acts on them. In vehicles, these forces come from the engine, brakes, and wheels.

Steam engines were the first form of power for vehicles. This steam car appeared in 1854.

THE FORCES ON A VEHICLE

Several different forces act on a vehicle as it moves. Thrust is the force created by the engine that pushes the vehicle forward. It works by the tires gripping on the road surface.

Two forces act in the opposite direction from thrust. They are drag, created by the air flowing past the vehicle as it moves, and friction, which tries to stop the vehicle's moving parts from sliding against each other.

Thrust created by the engine drives the vehicle forward.

CONTROLS

Electronic systems make vehicles safer and cheaper. They include anti-lock braking, engine management, and navigation systems (see page 20).

Because of gravity's pull the vehicle needs more power to go uphill than downhill. It also presses the tires onto the road.

BODY AND STRUCTURE

A vehicle needs a solid structure to support its heavy mechanical parts. A strong body also helps to protect passengers from injury (*right*).

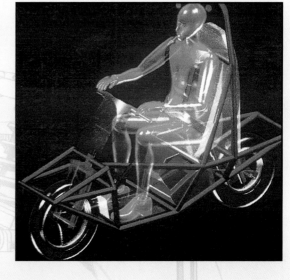

Drag slows down a moving vehicle.

Friction in the wheel bearings slows a vehicle down. See page 6 to find out why.

Gravity pulls the vehicle downward.

ENGINES AND MOTORS

Most vehicles have gasoline engines, where the fuel burns inside cylinders. The engine releases the energy stored in the fuel and uses it to make the vehicle move. Electric trains and some cars have electric motors instead of gasoline engines (see page 19).

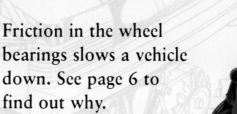

WHEELS

Wheels let a vehicle roll smoothly along. Their tires create friction with the road, causing traction (grip) for acceleration and for braking (*above*). Some trains are held clear of their tracks with magnets (*left*). This removes all friction with the rails (see page 7).

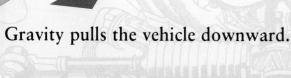

CHAPTER 1 – WHEELS

Friction is very important for vehicle designers. It is a force that tries to stop surfaces from moving against each other. A vehicle without wheels would create huge friction between itself and the ground. This would make it very difficult to move.

WHAT IS FRICTION?

Friction happens between two surfaces because bumps and hollows in the surfaces catch against each other. Even  smooth surfaces look quite rough under a microscope (*above*).

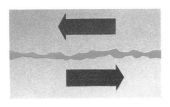 When slippery liquids, called lubricants, are put between the two surfaces, they separate them slightly. This stops the bumps from catching and reduces the friction. Moving parts in vehicles are usually lubricated with oil.

Another way of reducing friction is to put balls or cylinders between the surfaces. Only a small part of each ball touches the surfaces at one time, and this reduces friction.

AXLES AND BEARINGS

Wheels are firmly attached to a vehicle with an axle or a shaft. These help the wheels to turn freely because they are much thinner than a wheel – so there is a smaller surface to create friction.

The axle is supported inside a ring by balls. These reduce friction because they touch only a small part of the axle's surface.

Ball bearing

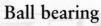

WHY WHEELS WORK

Wheels reduce friction because they roll with the movement of the vehicle, without any surfaces rubbing together. At the same time, they provide grip because of the friction between the tire and the road.

Maglev (short for magnetic levitation) trains are pushed clear of their tracks by magnets, which reduces the friction to zero.

Magnets

Magnets

Flange

TRAIN WHEELS

A train wheel is a solid steel disk. Wheels come in pairs on steel rods called axles. The axles are attached to the train with bearings. Each wheel has a lip (or flange) on the inside rim to stop it from slipping sideways off its rail.

MODEL CAR
PART 1
WHEELS

Add a rubber band to make tires

1 To make your car, start with the wheels. Trace eight part **A**s from the plans at the end of the book. Then cut them out from corrugated cardboard.

2 Glue two part **A**s together to make a front wheel. To make a back wheel, straighten out one half of a paper clip and poke it through a part **A**. Then glue another part **A** to it (*right*). Make two back wheels and two front wheels in all.

3 Cut a piece of dowel so that it is just wider than part **M** (see ends). Then glue a front wheel to one end.

4 Roll up a piece of cardboard so that it fits around the dowel, then glue it (*below*). Thread the dowel through and glue the other front wheel to it.

Dowel fits in here

SUSPENSION AND TIRES

If a vehicle's wheels were attached firmly to its body, the passengers would feel every bump that the vehicle went over. A suspension system allows the wheels to move up and down under the body, reducing the effect of the bumps.

To feel how a spring works, hop up then land without bending your knees. Can you feel the force? That's why you normally bend your knees, because they act like springs to give you a soft landing.

With a simple spring suspension, the vehicle would keep bouncing after going over a bump. A device called a damper prevents this.

3. Oil stops spring from bouncing back.

Make your own springs

Leaf spring

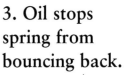

SPRINGS

When a spring is squashed, it stores energy, then releases it when it bounces back. Some springs are coils, others are made of curved plates of metal (called leaf springs). These work like a diving board, but bend in the middle.

 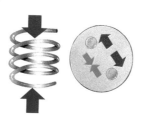

A spring also bounces back if it is stretched.

A spring shape will only work if it is made from an "elastic" material – one that returns to its original shape after being squashed or stretched.

AIR SUSPENSION

Some vehicles use air suspension. Instead of metal springs, air is squashed and expands inside a sealed cylinder.

Air

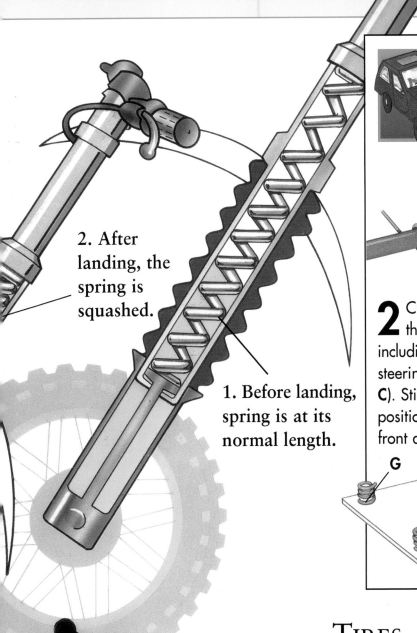

2. After landing, the spring is squashed.

1. Before landing, spring is at its normal length.

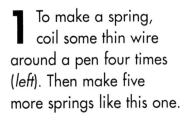

MODEL CAR
PART 2
SUSPENSION

1 To make a spring, coil some thin wire around a pen four times (*left*). Then make five more springs like this one.

2 Cut out part **B** from thick cardboard, including the hole for the steering wheel (marked **C**). Stick two springs at positions **D** and **E**. Then glue **B** to the front axle section you made on page 7.

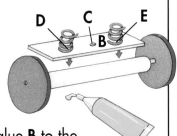

3 Cut out part **F** from thick cardboard and stick the other four springs onto it at positions **G**, **H**, **I**, and **J**, using strong glue.

SHOCK ABSORBERS
A shock absorber is a cylinder filled with thick oil that surrounds a piston connected to the wheel. After a spring is squashed going over a bump, the thick oil slows the piston down and stops the spring from bouncing back.

TIRES
A modern tire is made up of many layers. Inside is a tube filled with air that acts like a spring. The outside of the tire normally has a pattern of grooves. In wet weather, these stop the vehicle from slipping by letting water escape from between the tire and the road.

Wet weather tires

Racing cars use tires with no tread in dry conditions.

Rubber tread

Rayon

Steel band

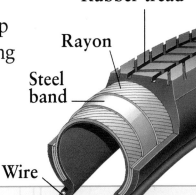

Wire

CHAPTER 2 – STRUCTURE

A car's body creates a space for the passengers and their luggage or cargo, and normally supports all the other parts of the car. The body needs to be a strong structure that protects the passengers and is rigid enough to support the weight of the engine.

It must also be as light as possible to let the car speed up quickly.

You can test how a car's crumple zone works. See the experiment on page 11.

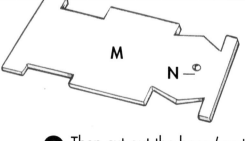

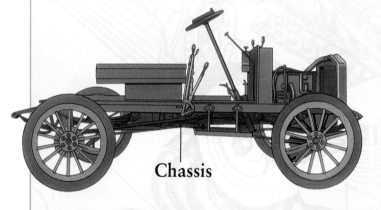

Chassis

Until the 1940s, most cars had a heavy metal chassis that supported the wheels and engine. The body, called coachwork, was built on top. This was often made from wood.

MODEL CAR
PART 3
THE BODY

1 Cut out the body (part **K**) from thin cardboard. Don't forget to cut out the hole for the steering (**L**). Then glue the body together using the tabs.

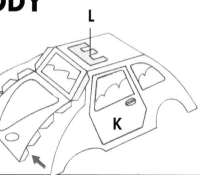

2 Then cut out the base (part **M**) from thick cardboard. Next, cut out the hole for the steering (**N**). You have now made the main sections – turn to page 17 to add the power!

MOTORCYCLES AND TRAINS

A motorcycle frame is made of metal tubes welded together to create a strong but light structure that supports all the other parts of the bike.

Trains are built more like old cars, with the body and engine sitting on a heavy chassis.

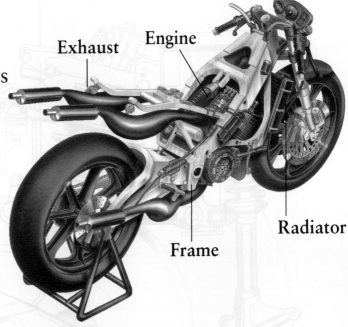

Exhaust Engine

Radiator

Frame

Monocoque structure

BODY SHELLS

Most cars are built around a single-piece metal shell called a monocoque. This is made from sheets of metal pressed into shape and welded together. Other body panels are connected to the shell by bolts and hinges.

Crumple Zones

Crumple zones are sections of a car's body that collapse in a collision, reducing the force of the impact. To see how they work, try this experiment.

1 Find a rectangular box. At one end, tape on a sheet of paper (or two) to make a tube. This makes a rigid crumple zone.

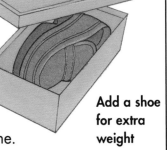

Add a shoe for extra weight

2 Drop the box onto a hard surface on the solid end and it will bounce after the hard impact. Now drop the box on its crumple zone, and the impact is absorbed as the tube crumples up.

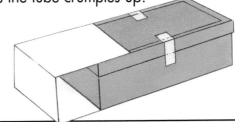

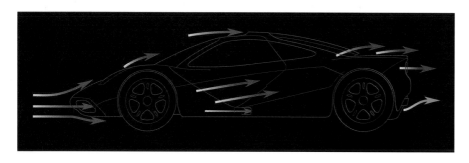

AIR FLOW

The more easily the air can flow around a vehicle, the smaller the drag on the vehicle. A car with good streamlining will go faster and use less fuel than a badly designed one.

STREAMLINING

Drag is the force that tries to slow a vehicle as it moves through the air. The faster the vehicle goes, the greater the drag gets. In fact, if the speed doubles, the drag becomes four times greater.

Eventually, drag gets as big as the thrust from the engine, stopping the vehicle from going any faster.

Streamlining is shaping the vehicle's body to reduce drag.

You can use a model car to test streamlining and drag for yourself.

SMOOTH TRAINS

Streamlining is important for all vehicles. High-speed express trains need careful streamlining at the front. Curved shapes allow the air in front of the train to flow smoothly over, under, and around.

HIGH-SPEED CARS

City cars hardly ever reach high speeds, so streamlining is less important than it is for cars designed for high-speed highway travel. Racing cars also have airfoils, parts that are shaped like a plane's wing. They push the car down, increasing its grip on the road.

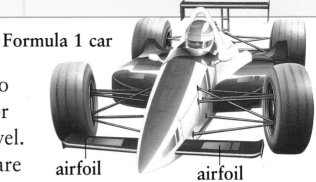

Formula 1 car

airfoil   airfoil

The smooth shape of these modern city cars helps them to use less fuel.

A racing bike has smooth body panels for extra speed.

Streamlining

Try this experiment to test streamlining.

1 Take an old toy car and drop it down the sloping end of a full bath (*bottom*). Place a coin on the bottom of the bath to mark how far it goes.

2 Then find a small, rectangular cardboard box that covers the outside of the car. Tape it over the car, then try sliding the car down the bath again. It won't go as far, because its shape is less streamlined.

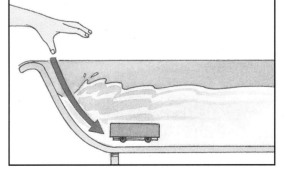

Motorcycles have a smooth front section called a fairing. This guides the air around the motorcycle. The rider can duck behind it to reduce drag, too.

BUILDING CARS

Most cars are built on automated production lines in huge factories. As each car body moves along the production line, workers and robots add parts, such as seats and doors. Engines are built on their own production lines before being fitted.

In some plants, robot vehicles deliver parts to the production line from the parts warehouse.

The car body is made from sheets of steel formed into shape by huge presses and welded together by robot welders.

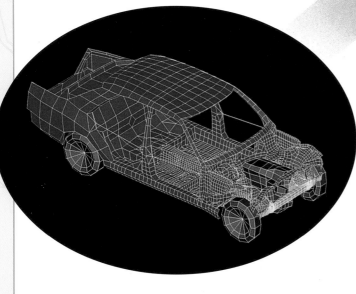

The first cars produced on a production line were made in the early 1920s by Henry Ford. They were a lot cheaper than cars built one by one.

DESIGN

The look of a new car is developed by a car designer. The thousands of parts are then designed on a computer.

Before the car is put on the road, full-size models and prototypes are tested for looks, safety, and performance.

Completed cars go through quality control, where they are tested to make sure everything is working properly.

CRASH TESTS

Crash tests demonstrate how well a new car model stands up to different sorts of crashes, such as front and side impacts. Crash-test dummies in the car contain sensors that measure the forces that passengers would feel in a crash.

The body and other panels are painted in an enclosed paint area. Many layers of paint protect the metal against rust.

The engine and transmission are assembled and attached to the body. Then carpets are laid on the floors and the seats are bolted down.

RECYCLING

Cars do not last forever. Many parts, such as brake pads and exhaust pipes, wear out after a few years and are replaced. Eventually, the body begins to rust and lose strength, and then the car is scrapped. Many metal and plastic parts (in green, *below*) can be recycled into new materials to make new cars.

Robots do a lot of the work in a modern factory. But humans are still very important in checking that the work has been done correctly.

CHAPTER 3 – ENGINES

The main picture shows how a single cylinder works. But most engines have from two to eight cylinders.

A vehicle's engine provides the energy needed to move the vehicle. The job of the engine is to convert the chemical energy stored in fuel into energy that makes the vehicle move.

It does this by burning fuel. This turns chemical energy into heat energy. The heat energy makes the burning gases expand inside a cylinder. The gases push against a piston, which turns the crankshaft.

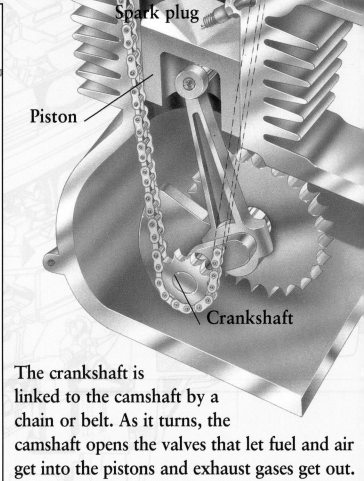

Camshaft

Exhaust out

Valves

Spark plug

Piston

Crankshaft

The crankshaft is linked to the camshaft by a chain or belt. As it turns, the camshaft opens the valves that let fuel and air get into the pistons and exhaust gases get out.

Power from Chemicals

In an engine, the pistons are moved by hot gases. These are created during a chemical reaction between fuel and air. In this experiment, gas released from chemicals is used to force your hands apart.

1 Pour four teaspoons of baking soda into an empty plastic bottle and fold the bottle tightly in half.

2 Pour a few teaspoons of vinegar into the bottle and put the top on. Squeeze the bottle between your hands and shake it to mix the chemicals. The reaction creates gas that fills the bottle, forcing your hands apart (*top*).

INSIDE A GASOLINE ENGINE

In a gasoline engine, fuel mixed with air burns inside the cylinders. The fuel burns in short bursts, making explosions that create hot gases. The gases push the pistons, which are linked to the gearbox by the crankshaft.

Waste gases are pushed out of the car through the exhaust system.

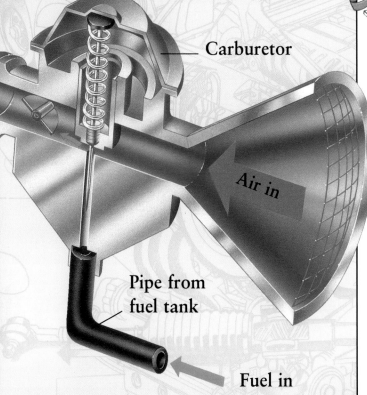

The mix of fuel and air is lit by a tiny spark from a spark plug (*left*) powered by electricity.

—— Carburetor

Air in

Pipe from fuel tank

Fuel in

FUEL AND AIR MIX

Fuel cannot burn without oxygen from the air. So it is mixed with air inside the carburetor before being sucked into the pistons.

MODEL CAR
PART 4
ENGINE

ADULT HELP NEEDED

1 Find a felt tip pen case and cut off the top and bottom so it is just wider than the rear wheel section (part **F**).

2 After this, ask an adult to cut a section 1 inch wide in the middle of the pen case. Then thread a thick rubber band through the case. Using strong glue, stick the case along the dotted lines on **F**.

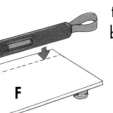

F

3 Take the rear wheels you made on page 7 and thread the end of the paper clip on each wheel through a bead (*below*). Then hook the paper clip ends around the end of the rubber band.

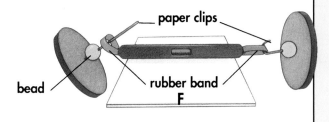

paper clips

bead

rubber band

F

4 After adding both wheels, pull the rubber band through the hole in the middle of the pen case. Keep pulling until the band is fairly tight and both beads are against the ends of the pen case, but aren't *too* tight (*left*). Then staple the band firmly to **F**.

F

5 Finally, use a strong glue to attach the springs on **F** to part **M**.

M

OTHER ENGINES

Most cars are powered by gasoline engines. But other types of engine are increasingly common. Diesel engines are often used in trucks, and electric motors are used in many trains.

Some engines are also designed to use unusual fuels, such as methane or hydrogen. A few high-speed, record-breaking cars have used jet engines.

You can feel how the air and fuel inside a diesel engine heat up as they are squashed. Hold a finger over the hole in a bicycle pump and push in the handle.

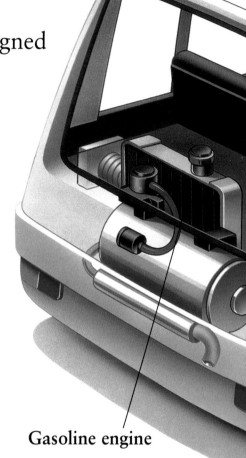

Gasoline engine

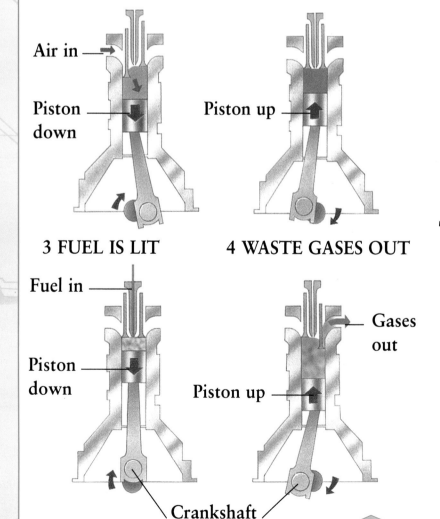

1 AIR SUCKED IN

Air in →

Piston down

2 PISTON SQUASHES AIR

Piston up →

3 FUEL IS LIT

Fuel in

Piston down

4 WASTE GASES OUT

→ Gases out

Piston up →

Crankshaft

THE DIESEL ENGINE

In a diesel engine, air inside the cylinders is compressed (squashed) by the pistons. This makes the air very hot.

Fuel is injected into the air, which is so hot that the thick diesel fuel explodes. This pushes the pistons down and drives the crankshaft around.

ELECTRIC MOTORS

HYBRID CAR

An electric motor turns electrical energy into movement (kinetic energy). Inside the motor, a coil of wire, called a rotor, has magnets around it. When electricity flows through the rotor, the magnets make it spin. The electrical energy comes from batteries, where it is stored as chemical energy. But most electric cars can only travel 60 miles before their batteries need charging again.

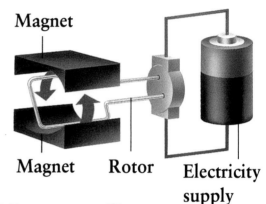

Magnet

Magnet   Rotor   Electricity supply

Electric motor

HYBRID CARS

Some cars have a gasoline engine *and* electric motors on each wheel. Batteries provide the electricity for the motors on short journeys.

On long journeys, where the batteries would run down, the engine drives a generator that produces electricity for the motors.

Electric locomotives get power from overhead electric cables, a third electric rail on the track, or a generator driven by a diesel engine.

Electric cables

ELECTRIC MOTOR

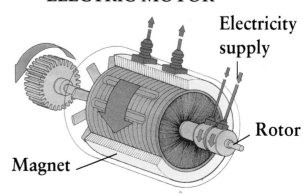

Electricity supply

Rotor

Magnet

Battery

Motors

CHAPTER 4 – CONTROLS

A driver uses simple controls (accelerator, clutch, and brake pedals, a gear shift and a steering wheel) to make a car speed up, slow down, and turn.

Many modern cars have complex electronic circuits that help the driver to drive safely and in comfort.

Add steering to your model.

TODAY'S CAR

We are just entering a new age where we have huge control over our car. In the first cars, levers and springs were used to apply controls. The latest cars combine computers and hydraulics.

Modern cars are also increasingly "green." Filters such as CATS (catalytic converters) cut out harmful gases that pollute the atmosphere.

The Mercedes A class, shown here, has a computer that makes the most efficient use of fuel at different speeds and controls the car's braking and balance.

Navigation

Stabilizing controls

Computer

Fuel injection

Anti-lock brakes

If a car stops violently, air bags inflate quickly to stop passengers from going through the windshield.

Air-conditioning systems keep the air inside the car at a comfortable temperature and humidity.

THE BEST ROUTE

In-car navigation systems guide drivers automatically to their destinations. They use a satellite navigation system to determine where the car is, and a database of roads to determine the best route. Some systems can also receive information about traffic jams and navigate around them.

Power steering

Exhaust system

NOT TOO CLOSE!

Some of the newest cars have a detection system that warns the driver if they are too close to the car in front, and applies the brakes to prevent the car from getting any closer.

A similar system warns the driver about objects in the way when the car is in reverse.

MODEL CAR
PART 5
STEERING

1 Push a bendy drinking straw through the holes in **M** and **B** and glue it to **B**. Cut out **O**, and glue this to the straw above **M** so that the springs on the front axle touch **M**, but **B** can still turn freely.

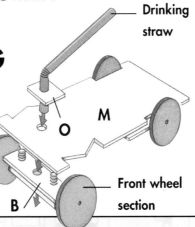

Drinking straw

O

M

B

Front wheel section

K

M

2 Now glue **K** to **M**. The straw should poke out of the top of **K**. Try the straw in different slots to steer the car.

Gear Systems

A car's transmission system carries the power from the engine to the wheels. It is made up of a gearbox (and normally a clutch) and driveshafts. The faster the engine turns, the more power it produces. Gears allow the engine to turn quickly whether the car is just starting off or speeding along.

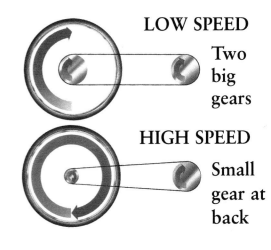

LOW SPEED
Two big gears

HIGH SPEED
Small gear at back

Two gears the same size spin at the same speed. But if one gear is twice as big as the other, the small gear will spin twice as fast.

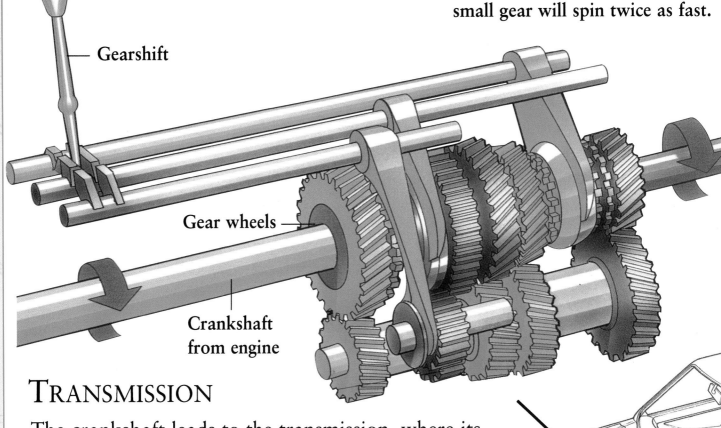

Gearshift

Gear wheels

Crankshaft from engine

Transmission

The crankshaft leads to the transmission, where its speed is reduced by the gear. The gearshift selects a set of gears that make the correct reduction for the car's speed. First gear makes the wheels turn very slowly for starting off. Higher gears make the wheels turn more quickly for driving. The clutch releases the gears from the engine. This allows a smooth change from one gear to another.

THE DIFFERENTIAL

The differential allows a pair of wheels being driven by the engine to turn at different speeds as a car turns a corner.

When a car drives straight, the small differential gears are carried around by the crown wheel. When a car turns corners, the differential gears spin the two driveshafts at different speeds.

Differential gearwheel

Driveshaft wheel

Crown wheel

Driveshaft from gearbox

Differential gearwheel

Driveshaft to wheel

When a car goes around a tight corner, the wheels on the outside of the corner have to travel farther than those on the inside.

Spur gears

Bevel gears

Rack and pinion gears

TYPES OF GEARS

Gear mechanisms are used to transfer power, normally from one spinning shaft to another. They can change the speed and direction of the rotation.

Spur gears are used when the shafts are parallel to each other. Bevel gears connect shafts at right angles. Rack and pinion gears connect a shaft with a straight surface that moves from side to side.

CHANGING SPEED AND DIRECTION

To accelerate, a vehicle needs more thrust. This is achieved by sending more fuel to the engine. To slow down, it needs more friction. This is achieved by using the brakes to increase the friction on the wheels. To steer around a curve, a vehicle needs a force acting on it toward the bend. In a car, this force comes from the friction of tires pushing sideways against the road.

Slide a ruler between your thumb and finger (*above right*). The tighter you grip the ruler, the greater the friction. This is how brakes work.

BRAKES

Brakes work by pressing pads against parts of the wheels. This creates friction that slows the wheels. But if the driver presses too hard on the brake pedal, especially on wet roads, the brakes "lock," making the wheels skid (*above*). An anti-lock braking system (ABS) detects if the wheels are about to skid and releases the brakes slightly.

In drum brakes, each wheel has a drum attached and brake pads press on its inside.

Drum

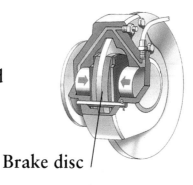

In disc brakes, each wheel has a metal disc attached and brake pads press on each side of it.

Brake disc

Around the Bend

Because trains run on tracks, the engineer does not need to steer. The force to make the train go around a curve comes from the track pushing sideways on the wheels. If a train turned too quickly, this force would tip it over. Tilting the train (or the track) helps to prevent this.

Motorcyclists lean over as they turn corners. This stops the sideways force on the tires from flipping the bike sideways.

The spinning wheels create a force at right angles to the bike.

Gravity pulls downward

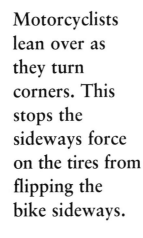

Spin Power

The gyroscopic effect of the spinning wheels helps motorcycles and bicycles stay upright when they are moving.

The same effect stops a spinning top from toppling over. Try making a top from a short pencil and circle of cardboard.

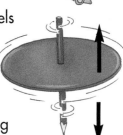

Forces at right angles to the spin

Racing car steering system

Car Steering

A normal car steering system uses a gear system called a rack and pinion to change the turning motion of the steering wheel into a sideways movement that twists the wheels from side to side. Turn to page 23 to see the special gears used for this.

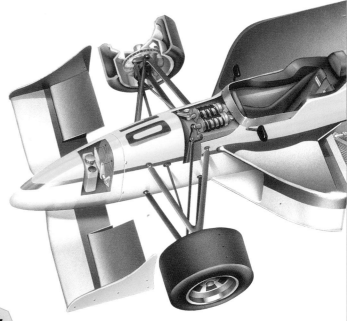

IN A COLLISION

Any moving object keeps on moving at the same speed unless something stops it or slows it down. This is what we call momentum.

If a car comes to a sudden stop, the driver and passengers continue to move because of this momentum. Only seat belts stop them from being thrown toward the front of the car.

KEEPING SAFE

A huge amount of research goes into making vehicles safer for travel. Vehicles have two types of safety systems – systems that help to prevent accidents, and systems that protect passengers if an accident occurs.

Emergency telephone

This new-style motorcycle has a lightweight, weatherproof body that protects the driver from wind and rain. The body is streamlined to reduce drag.

SIGNAL FOR SAFETY

Preventing collisions is especially important on railroads, where a single train can carry hundreds of passengers. Complex electronic circuits operate signals and switches. Automatic train protection systems on the trains themselves apply the brakes if the driver goes past a red light.

MODEL CAR
PART 6
PAINTING

1 Finish your car by painting it and adding pieces of tinfoil for the headlights.

2 To drive the car, wind up the rubber band by rolling the car backward along the floor.

The latest display systems project signs onto the inside of the windshield, where the driver can read them without looking away from the road.

:*50**

On highways, electronic signs warn of traffic congestion or fog. Signs are designed so they can be read quickly at high speeds.

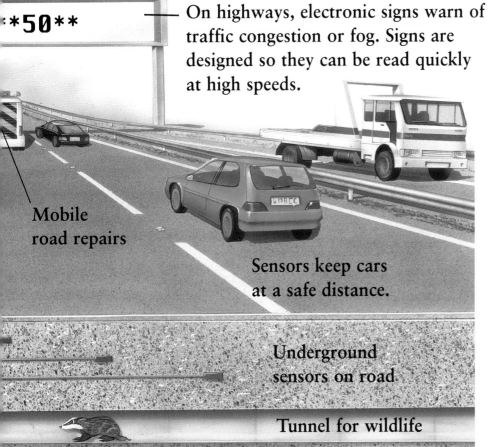

Mobile road repairs

Sensors keep cars at a safe distance.

Underground sensors on road

Tunnel for wildlife

No Hands!

In the future, cars might be able to drive themselves. Satellites will guide the cars and sensors will keep them a safe distance apart.

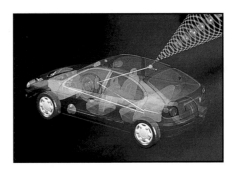

Difficult Driving

Bad weather, such as heavy rain, can make driving dangerous. Windshield wipers give the driver a better view and temperature sensors warns drivers that ice is likely to form on the road.

27

SCIENCE PRINCIPLES
LOOK BACK AND TEST YOUR KNOWLEDGE

SPEED AND ACCELERATION

Speed is the distance an object covers in a certain time, and is normally measured in feet per second or miles per hour. Acceleration is a measure of how quickly an object's speed is changing.

The word "acceleration" is normally used for speeding up, but slowing down is also acceleration (called deceleration), but in the direction opposite to motion.

? *(1) Which vehicle do you think normally accelerates faster, a car or a motorcycle?*

FORCE AND POWER

A force is a push or a pull. It has size and direction. Forces can cancel each other out. For example, in a car, thrust pushing forward can be equal to drag pushing backward. In science, power is different from force. It is the rate at which an engine produces energy.

? *(2) What has the most powerful engine – a car or a train? Answers to all questions are on page 32.*

DRAG AND FRICTION

Drag and friction are both forces. Drag is a force that acts on an object, when the object is moving through a fluid (a liquid or a gas), in the opposite direction to the movement. Friction is a force between two surfaces in contact with each other that tries to stop the surfaces from rubbing. The greater the force pressing the surfaces together, the greater the friction.

? *(3) Can you remember why a ball bearing reduces friction? (Turn to page 6 for help).*

HEAT ENERGY

Most energy can be turned easily into a different type of energy. Combustion, or burning, is when the chemical energy in a fuel is turned into heat energy.

Heat is also often "waste energy." Have you ever noticed how hot light bulbs get? This is because most of the energy from a candle or a light bulb is turned to heat.

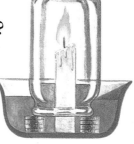

KINETIC ENERGY

Energy comes in two main forms. Potential energy (PE) is stored energy. Kinetic energy (KE) is the energy an object has because it is moving. On a swing, you are constantly changing between having KE and PE.

At the bottom of the swing, you are moving fastest, so your KE is at its greatest. By the time you swing up on the other side, your KE is zero, but your PE is at a maximum because of gravity. If it weren't for drag and friction, you'd swing forever.

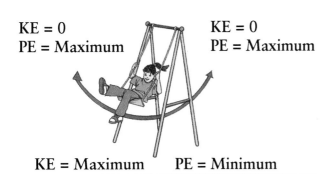

KE = 0
PE = Maximum

KE = 0
PE = Maximum

KE = Maximum   PE = Minimum

? *(4) Do you think the energy in fuel is a sort of kinetic energy or a sort of potential energy?*

ELASTICITY

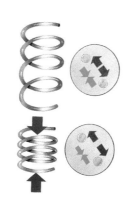

Most materials are elastic, if only a little bit. This means they will return to the same shape again after they have been bent or pulled by an outside force.

Metals are elastic, but they can be made to have more stretch by bending them into a spring.

TECHNICAL TERMS

Chassis — the supporting framework for the body, engine, and suspension in older cars.

Compression — decreasing the size of a gas, liquid, or solid, normally done by squashing them.

Corrosion — a chemical reaction between a metal, air, and water that gradually weakens the metal. Rusting is the corrosion of steel.

Expansion — an increase in size of a gas, liquid, or solid, usually because it is heated.

Generator — a device that creates electricity when its central core is spun around. It turns kinetic energy into electrical energy.

Lubricant — any substance that reduces the friction between two surfaces, such as oil or grease.

Recharging — putting electricity into a battery so that the battery can be used again after it has run down.

Sensors — devices that send information to a control system. In a car, sensors might measure the level in the fuel tank or the pressure of the lubricating oil in the engine.

Slicks — Tires with no tread.

Transmission — A system of shafts and gearboxes that transmits power from the engine to the axles.

Welding — to stick two pieces of metal together using melted metal.

VEHICLE PARTS

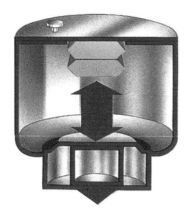

Cars and motorcycles may look different from one another, but they often have the same basic parts. Occasionally, new parts are invented, but constant developments make cars cheaper to make and more efficient to run.

1 ENGINE
The engine burns fuel to provide the thrust that moves a car forward.

2 CYLINDERS
Inside the engine are cylinders where the fuel burns. Most car engines have four cylinders.

3 PISTONS
Pistons move up and down inside the cylinders as the fuel burns. They turn a crankshaft that leads to the gearbox.

4 CLUTCH
A clutch disconnects the engine from the gearbox while the gears are changed.

5 TRANSMISSION
Gears, contained in the transmission, allow the wheels to turn at different speeds while it maintains the same engine speed.

6 DIFFERENTIAL
The differential is an arrangement of gears that allows the driving wheel to turn at different speeds as the car goes round a corner.

7 DRIVE SHAFT
The driveshaft carries power from the transmission to the wheels.

CAR SHAPES
A-D show some different car and motorcycle shapes. Which do you think are the most streamlined? Answers on page 32.

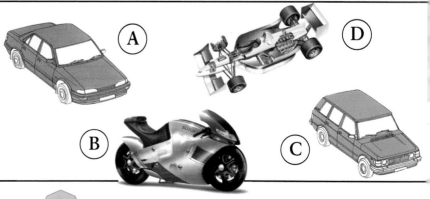

8 RADIATOR

Water is pumped through pipes inside the engine, cooling it down. The water gets hot and is cooled in the radiator.

9 SUSPENSION

A system of springs that allows a car's wheels to move up and down over bumps in the road.

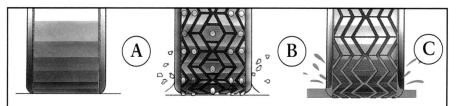

TIRES

Most car tires are designed to grip the road in normal conditions. But special tires are made for racing cars or rally cars. Can you figure out what tires **A-D**, shown here, are designed for?

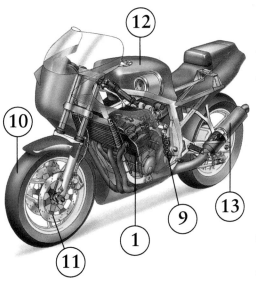

10 TIRES

Tires hold the road surface, providing traction and grip for braking.

11 BRAKES

Brakes create friction to slow a car. A hand brake stops the car from rolling when it is parked.

12 FUEL TANK

Where gasoline is stored.

13 EXHAUST SYSTEM

Waste gases formed by burning fuel in the engine are carried away into the air by the exhaust system.

14 BATTERY

The battery provides electricity for the motor that starts the engine and for lights and other electrical equipment when the engine is switched off.

15 DIESEL ENGINE

Some trains have powerful diesel engines to turn the electrical generators.

16 GENERATORS

When the generators are turned by the diesel engines, they produce electricity. This electricity powers the electric motors.

17 POWERED AXLE

Each axle has electric motors that turn it.

INDEX

The finished model car

Answers: Pages 28–29
1 A motorcycle usually accelerates faster than a car because it has a more powerful engine compared to its weight. **2** A train is more powerful than a car because it has to pull a heavier load.

3 Ball bearings reduce friction because they prevent surfaces from sliding against each other. **4** Fuel is chemical energy, which is a form of potential (stored) energy.
Page 30 B & D are the most streamlined shapes.

Page 31 Tire A is a slick – it is used for racing in dry weather. Tire B is has a thick tread, designed for off-road racing, Tire C has a normal tread, used in wet and dry conditions. Tire D has chains attached to it, for use in snowy conditions.

PHOTO CREDITS

Abbreviations – t – top, m– middle, b – bottom, r – right, l – left, c – center:
Pages 3, 13 both, 21 & 24-25 – Solution Pictures; 4, 14m, 20b & 24 – Mercedes Benz; 5t, 15t & br & 26 – BMW; 5b & 27 Frank Spooner Pictures; 14tl, m & bl – Ford UK; 20t – Volkswagen.

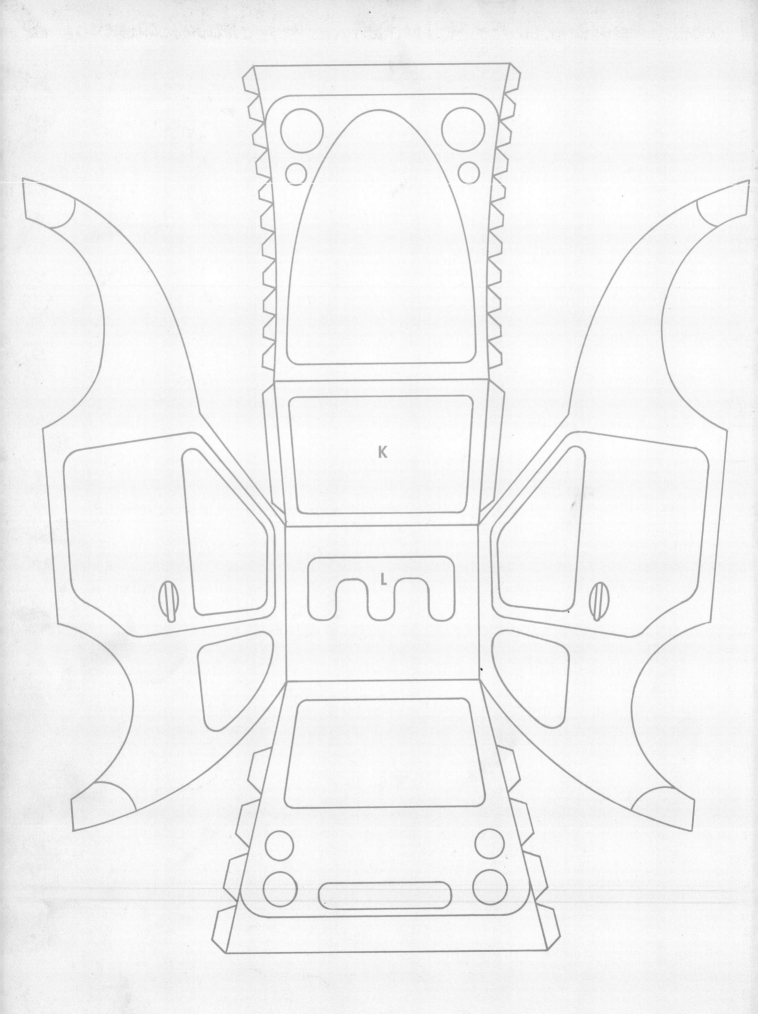